Cuneiform Spotlight of the Neo- and Middle Assyrian Signs

Norbert Gottstein and Strahil V. Panayotov

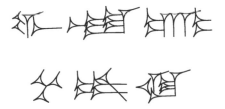

Norbert Gottstein and Strahil Panayotov
Cuneiform Spotlight of the Neo- and Middle Assyrian Signs

© Norbert Gottstein and Strahil Panayotov
© 2014 ISLET-Verlag, Dresden
Herstellung: Stephan Loschelders
Printed in Germany

ISBN 978-3-9814842-2-9

mail@islet-verlag.de
www.islet-verlag.de

Für Brigitte

Norbert Gottstein

За Мила

Strahil V. Panayotov

*Introduction**

The reading of cuneiform texts and the usage of sign lists has been developing continuously over more than 160 years. During this long stretch of time different sign lists were compiled. Still, to find a single sign in a list often takes a long time and it is especially difficult for beginners. Furthermore, a constant problem persists: how to order the cuneiform signs in a list? Thus, a stringent system allowing the user to spot a cuneiform sign easily has not yet been created. Modern sign lists use the Neo-Assyrian sign forms to build an ordered system. For instance, in the opinion of Rykle Borger (2010, xiii) it is virtually impossible to develop an ordered system for sign forms from the other periods. Thus, Borger partly changed the order of the signs in his last essential Zeichenlexikon.

The system presented here provides the possibility to find each sign swiftly. It can be applied to all sign forms consisting of wedges. The present list is based on sign shapes taken from existing lists of the Neo- and Middle Assyrian signs. Nevertheless, not all specimens are included. We tried to generalize the same shapes and not to repeat them. With a few exceptions the signs which occur only in the lexical lists are excluded. Every sign taken from an existing list is labeled with a siglum, shown in the footer of each page. References to numbers used in existing sign lists and other publications are provided by noting the numbers assigned to the signs in MZ$_2$ (Borger 2010), ABZ (Borger 1981) and AkkSyll (von Soden and Röllig 1991). The digital variant of the list, put together on paper by N. Gottstein, was improved and produced by S.V. Panayotov using InDesign.

The "Gottstein-System"

The system is based on what everybody knows in the field – the five elements of cuneiform script. They are the Grundelemente of the cuneiform (Borger 2010, xiii).

1)	vertical wedge	a
2)	horizontal wedge	b
3)	to the left falling wedge	c
4)	to the right falling wedge	d
5)	the Winkelhaken	e

The basic idea is to assign to each of these five elements its own name – a designation. The most simple and suitable names are the letters a, b, c and d. It is necessary that elements 3) and 5) are designated with the same letter c, in order to eliminate the confusion which occurs with these wedges. With the elements thus defined, the building of a system is a simple deduction. Nevertheless, letters as elements are not enough for precise specification of every single sign. Therefore, it is necessary to count every single element within a sign and then add the numbers to each letter in order to make an index. This leads to a quick identification of each sign. In this way signs can be ordered and spotted easily.

How to use the spotlight system

The example is based on a sign from category 9, EME, with the following parameters: a3b5c1.

the elements					Sign EME
designation	a	b	c	d	abc
parameters	sum of the designation and the indices				a3 b5 c1
category	number of elements				9 = 3+5+1

The sorting of the parameters follows the alphabet and is additionally combined with the indices. Thus to find the EME sign in the paper version you shall go to category 9, noted in the right upper corner of the list and then to a3b5c1. If you search for it in the PDF version or in another electronic format, you shall simply type a3b5c1 in the search box and you will find the sign immediately.

* We are thankful to Luděk Vacín for the English improvements. The logo on the front cover *pe-tu-ú sat-tak-ki* " unveiling cuneiform", an epithet of Asalluḫi, comes from the incantations *Utukkū Lemnūtu* Tablet 11, excerpt 4: 6, and is inspired by comunication with Mark J. Geller. See Geller 2007, 155

Advantages

There are several advantages of this system. It offers the possibility to spot fast and easily a cuneiform sign on paper and, which is innovative, on a computer screen. Thus, this is not a classical sign list but a system for tracing every shape of cuneiform signs. In this respect, it is not necessary to assign numbers to every sign and one can easily see and compare different shapes and signs from different periods. This was impossible with the other lists. The amount of wedges is decisive for a categorization of signs. This may be reminiscent of the syllabaries, where similar signs are listed together. Thus, the inner logic of the present system seems to be closer to the inner logic of the syllabaries, where different signs with the same amount of wedges were listed next to each other. For instance, in syllabary A the signs SUR (2) and PAD (3) consist of five wedges, BI (9) and NI (10) of four wedges, DA (65) and TA (66) of seven wedges, IB (160) and TAG (161) of five wedges, etc. (see Hallock 1955, 5-41). However, this ordering is not consecutive in the syllabaries and it is evident that the inner logic was not based only on such a system. Nevertheless, it is apparent that it played some role in the ancient ordering system, together with the shape of the signs or their syllabic values.

Furthermore, every single different sign can be easily inserted in the list and the system remains coherent. Therefore, the list is never finished and can grow over the time. These features make the system useful for paleographic projects.

Bibliography

BORGER, RYKLE (1981), *Assyrisch-babylonische Zeichenliste* (2. Auflage; Neukirchen-Vluyn: Verlag Butzon & Bercker Kevelaer).

-------(2010), *Mesopotamisches Zeichenlexikon. Zweite, revidierte und aktualisierte Auflage* (Alter Orient und Altes Testament, 305 (2. Auflage); Münster: Ugarit-Verlag).

CANCIK-KIRSCHBAUM, EVA C. (1996), *Die mittelassyrischen Briefe aus Tall Šēḫ Ḥamad* (Berichte der Ausgrabung Tall Šēḫ Ḥamad, Dūr-Katlimmu, 4/1; Berlin: Dietrich Reimer Verlag).

GELLER, MARKHAM J. (2007), *Evil Demons. Canonical Utukkū Lemnūtu Incantations: introduction, cuneiform text, and transliteration with a translation and glossary* (State Archives of Assyria Cuneiform Texts, 5; Helsinki: The Neo-Assyrian Text Corpus Project).

HALLOCK, RICHARD T. (1955), *Syllabary A* (Materialien zum sumerischen Lexikon, 3; Roma: Pontificium Institutum Biblicum).

JAKOB, STEFAN (2009), *Die mittelassyrischen Texte aus Tell Chuēra in Nordost-Syrien. Mit einem Beitrag von Daniela I. Janisch-Jakob* (Vorderasiatische Forschungen der Max Freiherr von Oppenheim-Stiftung, 2/3; Wiesbaden: Harrassowitz).

MAUL, STEFAN M. (1992), *Die Inschriften von Tall Bderi* (Berliner Beiträge zum Vorderen Orient, 2; Berlin: Dietrich Reimer Verlag).

POSTGATE, JOHN N. (2008), 'The Organization of the Middle Assyrian Army: Some Fresh Evidence', in Philippe Abrahami and Laura Battini-Villard (eds.), *Les armées du Proche-Orient ancien (IIIe-Ier mill. av. J.-C.): actes du colloque international organisé à Lyons les 1er et 2 décembre 2006, Maison de l'Orient et de la Méditerranée* (Oxford: John and Erica Hedges Ltd.), 83-92.

VON SODEN, WOLFRAM and RÖLLIG, WOLFGANG (1991), *Das Akkadische Syllabar* (Analecta orientalia, 42 (4., durchgesehene und erweiterte Auflage); Roma: Pontificium Institutum Biblicum).

WEIDNER, ERNST F. (1952-53), 'Die Bibliothek Tiglatpilesers I', *Archiv für Orientforschung*, 16, 197-215.

WIGGERMANN, FRANS A.M. (2008), 'A Babylonian Scholar in Assur', in Robartus J. van der Spek (ed.), *Studies in Ancient Near Eastern World View and Society: presented to Marten Stol on the occasion of his 65th birthday, 10 November 2005, and his retirement from the Vrije Universiteit Amsterdam* (Bethesda, Maryland: CDL Press), 203-34.

MZ$_2$	ABZ	AkkSyll	Sign	Name	Parameters
748 749	480	276	$\curlyvee$	DIŠ NIGIDA	a1
1	1	1		AŠ	b1
661	411	242		U	c1
575	360	209		GE23	c1

MA = MIDDLE ASSYRIAN FORMS AFTER ABZ AND MZ$_2$; NA = NEO-ASSYRIAN FORMS AFTER DITTO, ONLY NOTED WITH OTHER SIGLA; SH = CANCIK-KIRSCHBAUM 1996; TC = JAKOB 2009; TB = MAUL 1992; TP = WEIDNER 1952/3

MZ$_2$	ABZ	AkkSyll	Sign	Name	Parameters
753	532	287		ME	a1b1
750	481	277		LAL	a1b1
120 121 122	74 74, 100	47 48		MAŠ BAR BAN2	a1b1
824	534			DIŠ-U	a1c1
591	377	220		LIŠ	a1c1
869	545	296	MA	ŠU2	a1c1
825	570	308a		MIN	a2
839	579	311	TC	A	a2
847 848	585a			DIŠ/DIŠ NIGIDAMIN	a2
92	60	32	MA	PAB	b1c1
113 114	69	42	TC	BAD EŠE3	b1c1
112	75	49	TC	NU	b1d1
2 3	2	2		AŠ-AŠ HAL	b2
209	124	90		TAB	b2
92	60	32	MA	PAB	c1d1
576	362	210		GAM	c2
592	378			separator, gloss	c2
708	471	274		MAN	c2

MA = Middle Assyrian forms after ABZ and MZ$_2$; NA = Neo-Assyrian forms after ditto, only noted with other sigla;
SH = Cancik-Kirschbaum 1996; TC = Jakob 2009; TB = Maul 1992; TP = Weidner 1952/3

MZ$_2$	ABZ	AkkSyll	Sign	Name	Parameters
99	62	36	MA MA	SILA3	a1b1c1
125	74,355			GIDIM2	a1b1c1
157	90	67	SH	GAD	a1b1c1
379	230	145	MA	GAG	a1b1c1
596	381	221	MA	UD	a1b1c1
724	449	261		IGI	a1b1c1
10	13	12	TC	AN	a1b2
464 465	295	153		PA BANMIN	a1b2
469	296	156	TC TC	GIŠ	a1b2
379	230	145		GAG	a1b2
99	62	36	MA TC TC	SILA3	a1c1d1
596	381	221	TC	UD	a1c2
10	13	12	TC	AN	a1c2

MA = Middle Assyrian forms after ABZ and MZ$_2$; NA = Neo-Assyrian forms after ditto, only noted with other sigla;
SH = Cancik-Kirschbaum 1996; TC = Jakob 2009; TB = Maul 1992; TP = Weidner 1952/3

MZ$_2$	ABZ	AkkSyll	Sign	Name	Parameters
99	62	36		SILA3	a1c2
139	83	58		ŠITA3	a2b1
826	571			ŠUŠANA	a2b1
826	571			ŠUŠANA	a2c1
839	579	311		A	a3
850	585c			NIGIDAEŠ	a3
834	593			EŠ5	a3
865	598e			DIŠ/DIŠ/DIŠ	a3
9	12	11		TAR	b1c1d1
9	12	11		TAR	b2c1
672	420	244		AB2	b2c1
4	2a			EŠ6	b3
711	472	275		EŠ	b3
9	12	11		TAR	b3
210	124a			EŠ21	b3

MZ$_2$	ABZ	AkkSyll	Sign	Name	Parameters
505	325a			EŠ16	b3
839	579	311	MA MA	A	c2d1
470	296, 1			GUR17	c2d1
577	363			ILIMMU4 separator	c3
578	366	211	MA MA	KUR	c3
628	395	228		ZIB	c3
711	472	275		EŠ	c3
9	12	11	SH SH	TAR	c3

MA = MIDDLE ASSYRIAN FORMS AFTER ABZ AND MZ$_2$; NA = NEO-ASSYRIAN FORMS AFTER DITTO, ONLY NOTED WITH OTHER SIGLA;
SH = CANCIK-KIRSCHBAUM 1996; TC = JAKOB 2009; TB = MAUL 1992; TP = WEIDNER 1952/3

MZ$_2$	ABZ	AkkSyll	Sign	Name	Parameters
598	383	223	MA MA	PI	a1b1c1d1
598	383	223	TB MA	PI	a1b1c2
357	212	139	SH	IŠ	a1b1c2
118	73	46	MA	TI	a1b1c2
108	63a	37	MA / TB TB	KAD2	a1b1c2
94	60, 33	34	MA	BULUG3	a1b1c2
119	465	270	MA MA	DIN	a1b1c2
883	554	298		MUNUS	a1b1c2
14	5	4	TP SH / MA MA TC	BA	a1b1c2
110	70	43	MA / MA TC	NA	a1b1c2

MA = Middle Assyrian forms after ABZ and MZ$_2$; NA = Neo-Assyrian forms after ditto, only noted with other sigla; SH = Cancik-Kirschbaum 1996; TC = Jakob 2009; TB = Maul 1992; TP = Weidner 1952/3

MZ$_2$	ABZ	AkkSyll	Sign	Name	Parameters
118	73	46	MA	TI	a1b2c1
171	110	83a		KU7	a1b2c1
552	342	193	SH	MA	a1b2c1
736	457	266	TC	DI	a1b2c1
14	5	4	MA	BA	a1b2c1
110	70	43	MA SH TB	NA	a1b2c1
883	554	298	TC	MUNUS	a1b3
12	3	3	MA	MUG	a1b3
754	533	288	SH	MEŠ	a1b3
14	5	4	 MA SH	BA	a1b3
10	13	12	TC	AN	a1b3
110	70	43	MA SH	NA	a1b3

MA = Middle Assyrian forms after ABZ and MZ$_2$; NA = Neo-Assyrian forms after ditto, only noted with other sigla;
SH = Cancik-Kirschbaum 1996; TC = Jakob 2009; TB = Maul 1992; TP = Weidner 1952/3

MZ₂	ABZ	AkkSyll	Sign	Name	Parameters
552	342	193		MA	a1b3
548 549	339	192		AŠ2 BANEŠ	a1b3
110	70	43	TC	NA	a1c2d1
14	5	4	MA	BA	a1c2d1
110	70	43	SH / TC / TC	NA	a1c3
754	533	288	MA	MEŠ	a1c3
14	5	4	SH / SH / TC	BA	a1c3
612 613	393	226 227	MA	ERIM PIR2	a2b1c1
719	458			LAGAR	a2b1c1
132	78	52	MA / TC / TC TB	HU	a2b1c1
380	231	146	MA / TC	NI	a2b1c1
181	112	85	TC	SI	a2b1c1
755	483	280	MA	LAGAB	a2b1c1

MA = Middle Assyrian forms after ABZ and MZ₂; NA = Neo-Assyrian forms after ditto, only noted with other sigla; SH = Cancik-Kirschbaum 1996; TC = Jakob 2009; TB = Maul 1992; TP = Weidner 1952/3

MZ$_2$	ABZ	AkkSyll	Sign	Name	Parameters
827	574	309	MA MA	TUK	a2b1c1
380	231	146	TC	NI	a2b1d1
180	111	84		GUR	a2b2
181	112	85	MA	SI	a2b2
139	83	58		ŠITA3	a2b2
380	231	146		NI	a2b2
827	574	309		TUK	a2b2
751 752	482	278		LAL2 PAPNUN	a2b2
755	483	280		LAGAB	a2b2
849	585b			PAPNUN	a2c1d1
132	78	52	TC	HU	a2c2
380	231	146	TC	NI	a2c2
612 613	393	226 227		ERIM PIR2	a2c2
881	592	320	MA MA	SIG	a2c2

MA = Middle Assyrian forms after ABZ and MZ$_2$; NA = Neo-Assyrian forms after ditto, only noted with other sigla;
SH = Cancik-Kirschbaum 1996; TC = Jakob 2009; TB = Maul 1992; TP = Weidner 1952/3

MZ$_2$	ABZ	AkkSyll	Sign	Name	Parameters
755	483	280	SH / MA	LAGAB	a2c2
596	381	221	TB	UD	a2c2
143	87	63	MA / MA	NUN	a3b1
151	101	73	TB	SUR	a3b1
832	572			ŠANABI	a3b1
832	572			ŠANABI	a3c1
851 852 853	586	316		ZA LIMMU5 NIGIDALIMMU	a4
859 860	597	323	TC	NIG2 LIMMU	a4
117	72	45	MA	NUMUN	b1c2d1
117	72	45	MA / TC TC TC	NUMUN	b1c3
94	60, 33	34	MA	BULUG3	b1c3
632	396	230	MA	ŠAR2	b1c3
93	60, 24	33	MA	PUŠ2	b2c1d1
132	78	52	MA	HU	b2c2
632	396	230	MA	ŠAR2	b2c2

MA = Middle Assyrian forms after ABZ and MZ$_2$; NA = Neo-Assyrian forms after ditto, only noted with other sigla; SH = Cancik-Kirschbaum 1996; TC = Jakob 2009; TB = Maul 1992; TP = Weidner 1952/3

MZ$_2$	ABZ	AkkSyll	Sign	Name	Parameters
302	166	116		KASKAL	b2c2
358 359	214	140		BI EŠEMIN5	b2c2
94	60, 33	34		BULUG3	b2c2
93	60, 24	33		PUŠ2	b3c1
252	142	103	TC	I	b3c1
98	61	35	SH	MU	b3c1
701	444	259	SH	GIR3	b3c1
215	124, 42	91		LIMMU2	b4
506	325b			LIMMU4	b4
579	367	212	MA	ŠE	b4
711	472	275	MA	EŠ	b4
302	166	116	MA	KASKAL	c2d2
632	396	230	MA	ŠAR2	c2d2
94	60, 33	34	MA	BULUG3	c3d1
632	396	230	MA	ŠAR2	c3d1

MA = MIDDLE ASSYRIAN FORMS AFTER ABZ AND MZ$_2$; NA = NEO-ASSYRIAN FORMS AFTER DITTO, ONLY NOTED WITH OTHER SIGLA;
SH = CANCIK-KIRSCHBAUM 1996; TC = JAKOB 2009; TB = MAUL 1992; TP = WEIDNER 1952/3

MZ$_2$	ABZ	AkkSyll	Sign	Name	Parameters
628	395	228	MA	ZIB	c4
631 632 633	396	229 230 231		HI ŠAR2 TI2	c4
579	367	212	MA TC TC TC SH	ŠE	c4
854	379, 2			AD4	c4
712	473			NIMIN	c4
252	142	103	TC	I	c4
713	474			MAŠGI or BARAGI	c4

MA = Middle Assyrian forms after ABZ and MZ$_2$; NA = Neo-Assyrian forms after ditto, only noted with other sigla; SH = Cancik-Kirschbaum 1996; TC = Jakob 2009; TB = Maul 1992; TP = Weidner 1952/3

MZ$_2$	ABZ	AkkSyll	Sign	Name	Parameters
151	101	73	MA	SUR	a1b1c2d1
754	533	288	NA MA	MEŠ	a1b1c3
893	560	303a		NAGAR	a1b1c3
89	55	27	TC	LA	a1b1c3
94	60, 33	34	NA MA NA MA	BULUG3	a1b1c3
567	354	203	MA	ŠU	a1b2c1d1
118	73	46	MA	TI	a1b2c2
504	306	161	MA SH	UB	a1b2c2
690	433	251	MA	NIM	a1b2c2
472	297	159a		GU4	a1b2c2
514	330	180	MA NA	LU2*	a1b3c1
504	306	161	SH	UB	a1b3c1
550	340			BANLIMMU	a1b3c1
567	354	203	SH TC TC	ŠU	a1b3c1

MA = Middle Assyrian forms after ABZ and MZ$_2$; NA = Neo-Assyrian forms after ditto, only noted with other sigla;
SH = Cancik-Kirschbaum 1996; TC = Jakob 2009; TB = Maul 1992; TP = Weidner 1952/3

MZ₂	ABZ	AkkSyll	Sign	Name	Parameters
350	206	135		DU	a1b3c1
89	55	27	TC	LA	a1b3c1
223	128	93		AB	a1b4
552	342	193	MA	MA	a1b4
754	533	288		MEŠ	a1b4
553	343	194		GAL	a1b4
18	50	25	SH MA TC	ARAD	a1b4
89	55	27	MA	LA	a1b4
567	354	203		ŠU	a1b4
514	330	180	MA	LU2	a1b4
690	433	251	MA MA	NIM	a1c3d1
350	206	135	TC	DU	a1c4
589	376	218	SH MA	TE	a1c4

MA = Middle Assyrian forms after ABZ and MZ₂; NA = Neo-Assyrian forms after ditto, only noted with other sigla; SH = Cancik-Kirschbaum 1996; TC = Jakob 2009; TB = Maul 1992; TP = Weidner 1952/3

MZ$_2$	ABZ	AkkSyll	Sign	Name	Parameters
89	55	27	TC	LA	a1c4
567	354	203	TC	ŠU	a1c4
18	50	25	TC	ARAD	a1c4
754	533	288	TC	MEŠ	a1c4
357	212	139	TC TB	IŠ	a2b1c2
15	6	5	MA TC TP MA	ZU	a2b1c2
164	99	71		EN	a2b1c2
786	511	283	MA	TUL2	a2b1c2
669	417			U-GUR	a2b2c1
357	212	139	SH	IŠ	a2b2c1
736	457	266	MA	DI	a2b2c1
808 809 810 // 811	536	290 291	MA	KU TUG2 ŠE3	a2b2c1
483	307	162	TC	MAR	a2b2c1

MA = MIDDLE ASSYRIAN FORMS AFTER ABZ AND MZ$_2$; NA = NEO-ASSYRIAN FORMS AFTER DITTO, ONLY NOTED WITH OTHER SIGLA;
SH = CANCIK-KIRSCHBAUM 1996; TC = JAKOB 2009; TB = MAUL 1992; TP = WEIDNER 1952/3

MZ$_2$	ABZ	AkkSyll	Sign	Name	Parameters
870	546			EN2	a2b2c1
15	6	5	MA MA	ZU	a2b2c1
786	511	283		TUL2	a2b2c1
808 809 810 // 811	536	290 291	MA MA SH	KU TUG2 ŠE3	a2b3
127	97	70	TC	AG	a2b3
15	6	5	MA	ZU	a2b3
71	38	22	SH MA TC	URU	a2b3
483	307	162		MAR	a2b3
357	212	139	TC TB	IŠ	a2b3
15	6	5	MA	ZU	a2c2d1
746	469	273	MA	PAD	a2c2d1
164	99	71	SH	EN	a2c3
815	538	294	SH	KIN	a2c3

MA = MIDDLE ASSYRIAN FORMS AFTER ABZ AND MZ$_2$; NA = NEO-ASSYRIAN FORMS AFTER DITTO, ONLY NOTED WITH OTHER SIGLA; SH = CANCIK-KIRSCHBAUM 1996; TC = JAKOB 2009; TB = MAUL 1992; TP = WEIDNER 1952/3

MZ$_2$	ABZ	AkkSyll	Sign	Name	Parameters
736	457	266	TB	DI	a2c3
831	578a			2,30	a2c3
71	38	22	SH TC	URU	a2c3
357	212	139	TC	IŠ	a2c3
483	307	162	TC TC	MAR	a2c3
808 809 810 // 811	536	290 291	TC TB	KU TUG2 ŠE3	a2c3
760	486		TC	GIGIR	a2c3
437	232	147	MA SH	IR	a3b1c1
142	86	61	TC MA MA	RI	a3b1c1
153	103	75	MA NA	MUŠ3	a3b1c1
111	68	41	MA MA SH SH	RU	a3b1c1
495	324	174	TC	E2	a3b1c1

MA = Middle Assyrian forms after ABZ and MZ$_2$; NA = Neo-Assyrian forms after ditto, only noted with other sigla;
SH = Cancik-Kirschbaum 1996; TC = Jakob 2009; TB = Maul 1992; TP = Weidner 1952/3

MZ$_2$	ABZ	AkkSyll	Sign	Name	Parameters
172	104	76		SA	a3b2
174	105	77	TC	GAN2	a3b2
201	122	88	SH	MA2	a3b2
437	232	147	NA SH · SH	IR	a3b2
387 388	233 233, 22	148	NA MA	GA2 ŠITA	a3b2
807	535	289	SH	IB	a3b2
828	575	310		UR	a3b2
812 813	537	292 293	TC	LU DIB	a3b2
835	594	321		UR4	a3b2
495	324	174	TC · TB · TB	E2	a3b2
498	308	163		E	a3b2
484	313	166	TC · MA · MA	KID	a3b2

MA = MIDDLE ASSYRIAN FORMS AFTER ABZ AND MZ$_2$; NA = NEO-ASSYRIAN FORMS AFTER DITTO, ONLY NOTED WITH OTHER SIGLA; SH = CANCIK-KIRSCHBAUM 1996; TC = JAKOB 2009; TB = MAUL 1992; TP = WEIDNER 1952/3

MZ$_2$	ABZ	AkkSyll	Sign	Name	Parameters
490	318	169	MA / TC TC	U2	a3b2
201	122	88	TB	MA2	a3c2
599	384	224	SH	ŠA3	a3c2
498	308	163	TC	E	a3c2
837	593, 8-9			IŠŠEBU	a3c2
142	86	61	TC TC	RI	a3c2
484	313	166	TC	KID	a3c2
490	318	169	TC	U2	a3c2
151	101	73		SUR	a4b1
143	87	63	MA TB	NUN	a4b1
838	573			KINGUSILA	a4b1
151	101	73		SUR	a4c1
143	87	63	TB	NUN	a4c1

MA = MIDDLE ASSYRIAN FORMS AFTER ABZ AND MZ$_2$; NA = NEO-ASSYRIAN FORMS AFTER DITTO, ONLY NOTED WITH OTHER SIGLA; SH = CANCIK-KIRSCHBAUM 1996; TC = JAKOB 2009; TB = MAUL 1992; TP = WEIDNER 1952/3

MZ$_2$	ABZ	AkkSyll	Sign	Name	Parameters
745	468	272		KUG	a4c1
746	469	273		PAD	a4c1
856	589	317		HA	a4c1
859	597	323	TC · SH	NIG2	a5
861	598a	324		IA2	a5
634	405		MA	SUR3	b1c2d2
634	405		MA	SUR3	b1c3d1
98	61	35	SH · SH · SH · TB	MU	b1c4
634	405			SUR3	b1c4
580	371	213	SH · SH	BU	b1c4
634	405		MA	SUR3	b2c3
695	437	255		AMAR	b2c3

MA = Middle Assyrian forms after ABZ and MZ$_2$; NA = Neo-Assyrian forms after ditto, only noted with other sigla; SH = Cancik-Kirschbaum 1996; TC = Jakob 2009; TB = Maul 1992; TP = Weidner 1952/3

MZ₂	ABZ	AkkSyll	Sign	Name	Parameters
221	126	92	MA	TAG	b3c1d1
252	142	103	TC	I	b3c2
701	444	259		GIR3	b4c1
221	126	92	NA MA SH	TAG	b4c1
316	176			NINDA2	b4c1
562	350		MA	GAŠAN	b4c1
681	427	248		MI	b4c1
580	371	213	MA	BU	b5
513	329a			IA9	b5
252	142	103	SH	I	b5
216	125b			IA7	b5
711	472	275	MA	EŠ	b5

MA = MIDDLE ASSYRIAN FORMS AFTER ABZ AND MZ₂; NA = NEO-ASSYRIAN FORMS AFTER DITTO, ONLY NOTED WITH OTHER SIGLA; SH = CANCIK-KIRSCHBAUM 1996; TC = JAKOB 2009; TB = MAUL 1992; TP = WEIDNER 1952/3

MZ$_2$	ABZ	AkkSyll	Sign	Name	Parameters
857	590			ZUBUD HAtenû	c4d1
714	475			NINNU	c5
631	396	229	MA TC	HI	c5
298	167	117	SH	GAB	c5
98	61	35	TC TB	MU	c5

MA = MIDDLE ASSYRIAN FORMS AFTER ABZ AND MZ$_2$; NA = NEO-ASSYRIAN FORMS AFTER DITTO, ONLY NOTED WITH OTHER SIGLA;
SH = CANCIK-KIRSCHBAUM 1996; TC = JAKOB 2009; TB = MAUL 1992; TP = WEIDNER 1952/3

MZ₂	ABZ	AkkSyll	Sign	Name	Parameters
167	94	68		DIM	a1b1c3d1
130	76	50		MAŠ2	a1b1c4
5	9	8	SH / TC	BAL	a1b1c4
891	559	302		GU	a1b1c4
167	94	68	MA	DIM	a1b2c2d1
255	144	107	TC	TUR	a1b2c3
685	439	256	MA / TC / TC	PAN / see Postgate, 2008, 92	a1b2c3
698	441	258	TB	UL	a1b2c3
5	9	8	TC	BAL	a1b2c3
167	94	68	MA	DIM	a1b3c2
551	341			BANIA	a1b3c2
5	9	8	MA	BAL	a1b3c2
212	210	137a	NA MA	GEŠTIN	a1b3c2
230	132	98		URUDU	a1b4c1

MA = MIDDLE ASSYRIAN FORMS AFTER ABZ AND MZ₂; NA = NEO-ASSYRIAN FORMS AFTER DITTO, ONLY NOTED WITH OTHER SIGLA; SH = CANCIK-KIRSCHBAUM 1996; TC = JAKOB 2009; TB = MAUL 1992; TP = WEIDNER 1952/3

MZ$_2$	ABZ	AkkSyll	Sign	Name	Parameters
553	343	194	TC	GAL	a1b4c1
553	343	194	MA	GAL	a1b5
567	354	203	MA TC	ŠU	a1b5
255	144	107	MA	TUR	a1b5
258	145	108		AD	a1b5
270	146			HAŠHUR	a1b5
89	55	27	SH MA SH	LA	a1b5
90	56	28		APIN	a1b5
754	533	288	MA	MEŠ	a1b5
89	55	27	MA TC	LA	a1c5
721	459a	268	TB	DU6	a1c5
16	7	6	MA MA SH TB TC SH	SU	a2b1c3

MA = Middle Assyrian forms after ABZ and MZ$_2$; NA = Neo-Assyrian forms after ditto, only noted with other sigla;
SH = Cancik-Kirschbaum 1996; TC = Jakob 2009; TB = Maul 1992; TP = Weidner 1952/3

MZ₂	ABZ	AkkSyll	Sign	Name	Parameters
896	562	304		KUŠU2	a2b1c3
85	59	31	TC	LI	a2b1c3
136	80	55	MA / MA MA TB	IG	a2b1c3
815	538	294	TC	KIN	a2b1c3
693	435	254	MA	LAM	a2b2c2
378	228	142		KIB	a2b2c2
737	461	269	MA	KI	a2b2c2
474	298	160	TC TC	AL	a2b2c2
760	486		MA	GIGIR	a2b2c2
756	484		MA	ENGUR	a2b2c2
566	353	202	TC	ŠA	a2b3c1
474	298	160	MA	AL	a2b3c1

MA = Middle Assyrian forms after ABZ and MZ₂; NA = Neo-Assyrian forms after ditto, only noted with other sigla;
SH = Cancik-Kirschbaum 1996; TC = Jakob 2009; TB = Maul 1992; TP = Weidner 1952/3

MZ$_2$	ABZ	AkkSyll	Sign	Name	Parameters
561	335	191		DA	a2b3c1
737	461	269		KI	a2b3c1
756	484			ENGUR	a2b3c1
760	486			GIGIR	a2b3c1
875	548			GIBIL2	a2b3c1
16	7	6		SU	a2b3c1
756	484			ENGUR	a2b4
127	97	70		AG	a2b4
808 809 810 // 811	536	290 291		KU TUG2 ŠE3	a2b4
474	298	160		AL	a2b4
378	228	142		KIB	a2b4
511	328	178		RA	a2b4
464	295b			PA-AN	a2b4

MA = MIDDLE ASSYRIAN FORMS AFTER ABZ AND MZ$_2$; NA = NEO-ASSYRIAN FORMS AFTER DITTO, ONLY NOTED WITH OTHER SIGLA;
SH = CANCIK-KIRSCHBAUM 1996; TC = JAKOB 2009; TB = MAUL 1992; TP = WEIDNER 1952/3

MZ$_2$	ABZ	AkkSyll	Sign	Name	Parameters
561	335	191	TC	DA	a2b4
16	7	6	MA	SU	a2b4
20	52		TB MA	ITI	a2b4
246	129	94		NAB	a2b4
16	7	6	SH MA	SU	a2c3d1
808 809 810 // 811	536	290 291	TC	KU TUG2 ŠE3	a2c4
737	461	269	TC TB	KI	a2c4
760	486		TC TC	GIGIR	a2c4
566	353	202	TC	ŠA	a2c4
731	455	264	TB	U3	a2c4
148 149	88	64 65	MA MA	KAB HUB2	a3b1c2
111	68	41	SH MA TB SH TC	RU	a3b1c2
748	480	276		DIŠ+EN	a3b1c2

MA = Middle Assyrian forms after ABZ and MZ$_2$; NA = Neo-Assyrian forms after ditto, only noted with other sigla;
SH = Cancik-Kirschbaum 1996; TC = Jakob 2009; TB = Maul 1992; TP = Weidner 1952/3

MZ₂	ABZ	AkkSyll	Sign	Name	Parameters
111	68	41	MA	RU	a3b2c1
248	139	102	MA NA MA	TA	a3b2c1
812 813	537	292 293	MA	LU DIB	a3b2c1
438	280+249b	151 152	SH	DAG	a3b2c1
699	442			ŠITA4	a3b2c1
381	211	138	MA	UŠ	a3b2c1
494	321	172		LUH see Wiggermann, Fs. Stol, 230	a3b2c1
6 7	10	9	MA	GIR2 GIR2(gunû)	a3b2c1
559	349	199	TB	BUR	a3b3
13	4		MA	ZADIM	a3b3
438	280+249b	151 152	SH	DAG	a3b3
80	49*	24	MA	GIŠGAL	a3b3
485 486	314	167 168	SH	ŠID MES	a3b3
812 813	537	292 293	MA TC	LU DIB	a3b3
494	321	172	SH	LUH	a3c3

MA = MIDDLE ASSYRIAN FORMS AFTER ABZ AND MZ₂; NA = NEO-ASSYRIAN FORMS AFTER DITTO, ONLY NOTED WITH OTHER SIGLA; SH = CANCIK-KIRSCHBAUM 1996; TC = JAKOB 2009; TB = MAUL 1992; TP = WEIDNER 1952/3

MZ₂	ABZ	AkkSyll	Sign		Name	Parameters
485 486	314	167 168	SH	TC	ŠID MES	a3c3
812 813	537	292 293	TB	TC	LU DIB	a3c3
173	104, 6		MA	MA	AŠGAB	a4b1c1
496	322	173	SH		KAL	a4b1c1
11	14		MA		AŠ+ŠUR	a4b1c1
437	232	147	SH		IR	a4b1c1
495	324	174	SH		E2	a4b1c1
490	318	169	TC	SH	U2	a4b1d1
172	104	76	MA		SA	a4b2
173	104, 6				AŠGAB	a4b2
438	280+249b	151 152	SH		DAG	a4b2
11	14				AŠ+ŠUR	a4b2
496	322	173	MA		KAL	a4b2

MA = Middle Assyrian forms after ABZ and MZ₂; NA = Neo-Assyrian forms after ditto, only noted with other sigla;
SH = Cancik-Kirschbaum 1996; TC = Jakob 2009; TB = Maul 1992; TP = Weidner 1952/3

MZ₂	ABZ	AkkSyll	Sign	Name	Parameters
495	324	174	MA SH TC	ᴇ2 see Wiggermann, Fs. Stol, 230	a4b2
174 175	105	77 78		ɢᴀɴ2 ᴋᴀʀ2	a4b2
207	123	89	MA MA	ᴅɪʀ	a4b2
490	318	169	MA	ᴜ2	a4b2
173	104, 6		MA	ᴀšɢᴀʙ	a4c1d1
496	322	173	TC	ᴋᴀʟ	a4c2
495	324	174	TC	ᴇ2	a4c2
175	105	78	MA	ᴋᴀʀ2	a4c2
151	101	73	TC SH	sᴜʀ	a5b1
153	103	75	NA MA	ᴍᴜš3	a5b1
746	469	273	SH	ᴘᴀᴅ	a5b1
746	469	273	TC	ᴘᴀᴅ	a5c1
747	470			15	a5c1

MA = Mɪᴅᴅʟᴇ Assʏʀɪᴀɴ ꜰᴏʀᴍs ᴀꜰᴛᴇʀ ABZ ᴀɴᴅ MZ₂; NA = Nᴇᴏ-Assʏʀɪᴀɴ ꜰᴏʀᴍs ᴀꜰᴛᴇʀ ᴅɪᴛᴛᴏ, ᴏɴʟʏ ɴᴏᴛᴇᴅ ᴡɪᴛʜ ᴏᴛʜᴇʀ sɪɢʟᴀ; SH = Cᴀɴᴄɪᴋ-Kɪʀsᴄʜʙᴀᴜᴍ 1996; TC = Jᴀᴋᴏʙ 2009; TB = Mᴀᴜʟ 1992; TP = Wᴇɪᴅɴᴇʀ 1952/3

MZ₂	ABZ	AkkSyll	Sign	Name	Parameters
862	598b	325		AŠ3	a6
839	579a	315		A-A	a6
845	583			EDURU	a6
309	170	120	TC	AM	b1c5
665	415			UDUN	b1c5
640	406	235		KAM	b1c5
580	371	213	MA	BU	b1c5
338	190k		NA MA	GALAM	b2c3d1
678	425	247		KIŠ	b2c4
298	167	117	MA TC	GAB	b2c4
309	170	120	NA TB	AM	b2c4
115	71	44		ŠIR	b3c2d1
298	167	117	SH	GAB	b3c3
338	190k		NA MA	GALAM	b4c2
115	71	44	MA	ŠIR	b5c1

MA = Middle Assyrian forms after ABZ and MZ₂; NA = Neo-Assyrian forms after ditto, only noted with other sigla;
SH = Cancik-Kirschbaum 1996; TC = Jakob 2009; TB = Maul 1992; TP = Weidner 1952/3

MZ$_2$	ABZ	AkkSyll	Sign	Name	Parameters
536	331a			Aš9	b6
253 254	143	105 106		GAN KAM2	b6
217	125c			Aš4	b6
254	143	106	SH · TC	KAM2	c6
595	406	235		KAM*	c6
309	170	120	TC	AM	c6
715				60	c6

MZ$_2$	ABZ	AkkSyll	Sign	Name	Parameters
667	415a			GAKKUL3	a1b1c4d1
890	558	303		GEME2	a1b1c5
721	459a	268	TB	DU6	a1b1c5
514	330	180	TC	LU2	a1b1c5
353	208		TC	ANŠE	a1b2c1d3
504	306	161	MA	UB	a1b2c3d1
170	109	82		LAL3	a1b2c4
635	397	233		A'	a1b2c4
682	429	249	TC TC	GUL	a1b3c3
535	331	182	MA NA	ŠEŠ*	a1b3c3
720	459	267	MA MA	DUL	a1b4c2
900 901	565	307		LUM MURGU2	a1b4c2
376	226			GISAL	a1b4c2
296	130	96	TC	UG	a1b4c2
353	208		TC	ANŠE	a1b4c2

MA = Middle Assyrian forms after ABZ and MZ$_2$; NA = Neo-Assyrian forms after ditto, only noted with other sigla; SH = Cancik-Kirschbaum 1996; TC = Jakob 2009; TB = Maul 1992; TP = Weidner 1952/3

MZ$_2$	ABZ	AkkSyll	Sign	Name	Parameters
504	306	161		UB	a1b4c2
682	429	249		GUL	a1b4c2
564	351	200		SIG7	a1b5c1
683	430			GIR4	a1b5c1
353	208		SH SH	ANŠE	a1b5c1
252	142		TC	I+NA	a1b6
270	146		MA MA	HAŠUR	a1b6
89	55	27	TC	LA	a1b6
553	343	194	TC	GAL	a1b6
570	355	207	MA MA	LUL	a1b6
567	354	203	TC	ŠU	a1b6
258	145	108	SH SH	AD	a1b6
721	459a	268	TB	DU6	a1c6

MA = Middle Assyrian forms after ABZ and MZ$_2$; NA = Neo-Assyrian forms after ditto, only noted with other sigla; SH = Cancik-Kirschbaum 1996; TC = Jakob 2009; TB = Maul 1992; TP = Weidner 1952/3

MZ$_2$	ABZ	AkkSyll	Sign	Name	Parameters
641	399	236	NA TC MA	IM	a2b1c4
815	538	294	TC TC	KIN	a2b1c4
348	205	134	TC	IL	a2b1c2d2
348	205	134	TC TC	IL	a2b1c4
140	84	59	TC	ZI	a2b1c4
514	330	180	TC	LU2	a2b1c4
141	85	60	TC	GI	a2b1c4
16	7	6	SH	SU	a2b1c4
788	515	284	MA	BUL	a2b1c4
134	79	54	TC	NAM	a2b1c4
670	418		TC	U-DAR	a2b2c3
169	96			BULUG	a2b2c3
686	440	257	MA MA	GIM	a2b2c3

MZ$_2$	ABZ	AkkSyll	Sign	Name	Parameters
24	15	15	SH TC	KA	a2b2c3
566	353	202	SH	ŠA	a2b2c3
788	515	284		BUL	a2b2c3
737	461	269	SH	KI	a2b3c2
348	205	134	SH TC SH	IL	a2b3c2
561	335	191	SH	DA	a2b3c2
815	538	294	TC	KIN	a2b3c2
127	97	70	MA	AG	a2b3c2
24	15	15	TC	KA	a2b3c2
511	328	178	SH	RA	a2b3c2
566	353	202	SH TC	ŠA	a2b3c2
721	459a	268		DU6	a2b4c1
566	353	202	TC TC	ŠA	a2b4c1

MA = Middle Assyrian forms after ABZ and MZ$_2$; NA = Neo-Assyrian forms after ditto, only noted with other sigla; SH = Cancik-Kirschbaum 1996; TC = Jakob 2009; TB = Maul 1992; TP = Weidner 1952/3

MZ₂	ABZ	AkkSyll	Sign	Name	Parameters
737	461	269		KI	a2b4c1
561	335	191	SH TC TB MA	DA	a2b4c1
341	203	131		UR2	a2b4c1
24	15	15	TC	KA	a2b4c1
127	97	70	TC TB	AG	a2b4c1
808 809 810 // 811	536	290 291	MA	KU TUG2 ŠE3	a2b5
362	215	141	TC	ŠIM	a2b5
511	328	178	TC MA TB	RA	a2b5
259	147	109		ZI2	a2b5
292	164	115		SUM	a2b5
24	15	15	SH TC SH TB	KA	a2b5
256	144			TUR-DIŠ	a2b5

MA = Middle Assyrian forms after ABZ and MZ₂; NA = Neo-Assyrian forms after ditto, only noted with other sigla; SH = Cancik-Kirschbaum 1996; TC = Jakob 2009; TB = Maul 1992; TP = Weidner 1952/3

MZ₂	ABZ	AkkSyll	Sign	Name	Parameters
20	52		SH · · · SH	ITI	a2b5
127	97	70		AG	a2b5
16	7	6	SH	SU	a2c4d1
127	97	70	TC	AG	a2c5
808 809 810 // 811	536	290 291	TB	KU TUG2 ŠE3	a2c5
292	164	115	SH · · · SH	SUM	a2c5
20	52		TC	ITI	a2c5
90	56	28	TC	APIN	a2c5
85	59	31	SH · · · TC · · · TC	LI	a2c5
737	461	269	TC · · · TB	KI	a2c5
140	84	59	SH	ZI	a2c5
566	353	202	TC · · · TC	ŠA	a2c5

MA = Middle Assyrian forms after ABZ and MZ₂; NA = Neo-Assyrian forms after ditto, only noted with other sigla; SH = Cancik-Kirschbaum 1996; TC = Jakob 2009; TB = Maul 1992; TP = Weidner 1952/3

MZ$_2$	ABZ	AkkSyll	Sign	Name	Parameters
24	15	15	SH TC	KA	a2c5
731	455	264	TB	U3	a2c5
729	454		NA MA TC	SIG5	a3b1c3
248	139	102	SH SH	TA	a3b1c3
242	138	101	TC	DUB	a3b1c3
150	89	66	MA	HUB	a3b1c3
514	330	180	SH	LU2	a3b1c3
150	89	66	MA	HUB	a3b2c2
499	309	164		DUG	a3b2c2
804	529	286	MA	NIGIN	a3b2c2
222	133	99	MA	KA2	a3b2c2
238	134	100	TC	UM	a3b2c2
248	139	102	MA SH TC	TA	a3b2c2

MA = MIDDLE ASSYRIAN FORMS AFTER ABZ AND MZ$_2$; NA = NEO-ASSYRIAN FORMS AFTER DITTO, ONLY NOTED WITH OTHER SIGLA;
SH = CANCIK-KIRSCHBAUM 1996; TC = JAKOB 2009; TB = MAUL 1992; TP = WEIDNER 1952/3

MZ₂	ABZ	AkkSyll	Sign	Name	Parameters
491	319	170	TB	GA	a3b2c2
184	115	87	TC	SAG	a3b2c2
242	138	101	TC	DUB	a3b3c1
96	60			PA5 (PAB-E)	a3b3c1
745	468	272	TC	KUG	a3b3c1
184	115	87	MA MA SH MA	SAG	a3b3c1
73	40			UKKIN	a3b4
260	142a	104	SH	IA	a3b4
435 436	249 231	149		KISAL I3+GIŠ	a3b4
804	529	286		NIGIN	a3b4
438	280+249b	151 152	SH	DAG	a3b4
812 813	537	292 293		LU DIB	a3b4
184	115	87		SAG	a3b4
242	138	101	TC SH SH	DUB	a3b4

MA = Middle Assyrian forms after ABZ and MZ₂; NA = Neo-Assyrian forms after ditto, only noted with other sigla; SH = Cancik-Kirschbaum 1996; TC = Jakob 2009; TB = Maul 1992; TP = Weidner 1952/3

MZ$_2$	ABZ	AkkSyll	Sign	Name	Parameters
222	133	99		KA2	a3b4
745	468	272	TC	KUG	a3b4
238	134	100	MA MA	UM	a3b4
248	139	102		TA	a3b4
490	318	169		U2	a3b4
109	63c	38	MA	KAD3	a3c3d1
248	139	102	SH SH TB TC	TA	a3c4
745	468	272	MA	KUG	a3c4
729	454		TC	SIG5	a3c4
499	309	164	TC	DUG	a3c4
731	455	264	TB	U3	a3c4
631	404	241		HI-A	a3c4

MA = MIDDLE ASSYRIAN FORMS AFTER ABZ AND MZ$_2$; NA = NEO-ASSYRIAN FORMS AFTER DITTO, ONLY NOTED WITH OTHER SIGLA;
SH = CANCIK-KIRSCHBAUM 1996; TC = JAKOB 2009; TB = MAUL 1992; TP = WEIDNER 1952/3

MZ$_2$	ABZ	AkkSyll	Sign	Name	Parameters
812 813	537	292 293	TB TB	LU DIB	a3c4
238	134	100	TC	UM	a3c4
742	461, 280+464	269a	TC	KIMIN	a3c4
111	68	41	MA	RU	a4b1c2
494	321	172	MA	LUH	a4b2c1
731	455	264	TC	U3	a4b2c1
381	211	138	SH	UŠ	a4b2c1
559	349	199		BUR	a4b3
80	49*	24		GIŠGAL	a4b3
795	522	285	MA	SUG	a5b1c1
207	123	89	MA	DIR	a5b2
496	322	173	TC	KAL	a5b2
438	280+249b	151 152		DAG	a5b2
500 501	312	165	MA	KALAM UN	a5b2

MA = Middle Assyrian forms after ABZ and MZ$_2$; NA = Neo-Assyrian forms after ditto, only noted with other sigla; SH = Cancik-Kirschbaum 1996; TC = Jakob 2009; TB = Maul 1992; TP = Weidner 1952/3

MZ$_2$	ABZ	AkkSyll	Sign	Name	Parameters
795	522	285		SUG	a5b2
863 866	598c		MA, MA	IMIN	a7
640	406	235	SH, TC	KAM	b1c6
304	166b			ILLAT	b2c5
298	167	117	SH	GAB	b2c5
339	191	129	TC	KUM	b2c5
309	170	120	MA, TC	AM	b2c5
562	350		MA	GAŠAN	b3c4
543	333	186		GAR3	b3c4
339	191	129	TC	KUM	b3c4
339	191	129	MA, TC	KUM	b4c3
540	332	185	MA	ZAG	b6c1
684	428			ŠAGAN	b6c1

MA = MIDDLE ASSYRIAN FORMS AFTER ABZ AND MZ$_2$; NA = NEO-ASSYRIAN FORMS AFTER DITTO, ONLY NOTED WITH OTHER SIGLA;
SH = CANCIK-KIRSCHBAUM 1996; TC = JAKOB 2009; TB = MAUL 1992; TP = WEIDNER 1952/3

MZ$_2$	ABZ	AkkSyll	Sign	Name	Parameters
537	331b			IMIN3	b7
218	125d			IMIN2	b7
304	166b		MA	ILLAT	c5d2
562	350		MA NA	GAŠAN*	c7

MA = MIDDLE ASSYRIAN FORMS AFTER ABZ AND MZ$_2$; NA = NEO-ASSYRIAN FORMS AFTER DITTO, ONLY NOTED WITH OTHER SIGLA;
SH = CANCIK-KIRSCHBAUM 1996; TC = JAKOB 2009; TB = MAUL 1992; TP = WEIDNER 1952/3

MZ$_2$	ABZ	AkkSyll	Sign	Name	Parameters
296	130	96	TC	UG	a1b2c4d1
635	397	233	MA	A'	a1b2c5
252	142		TC	I+NA	a1b3c4
86 87 88	58	30 30a	MA · MA	TU KU4 GUR8	a1b3c4
644	401	238	SH	HAR	a1b3c4
560	334	187	SH	A2	a1b3c4
560	334	187	TB	A2	a1b4c3
19	51	25a		ARAD2	a1b4c3
232	195		MA	UNUG	a1b4c3
353	208		TC	ANŠE	a1b4c3
296	130	96	SH · TC	UG	a1b5c2
252	142		TB	I+NA	a1b5c2
353	208		MA · MA TC	ANŠE	a1b6c1

MA = MIDDLE ASSYRIAN FORMS AFTER ABZ AND MZ$_2$; NA = NEO-ASSYRIAN FORMS AFTER DITTO, ONLY NOTED WITH OTHER SIGLA; SH = CANCIK-KIRSCHBAUM 1996; TC = JAKOB 2009; TB = MAUL 1992; TP = WEIDNER 1952/3

MZ₂	ABZ	AkkSyll	Sign	Name	Parameters
354	207	137		TUM	a1b6c1
320	178aa	125	SH	ŠAM3	a1b6c1
351	201	132		SUHUŠ	a1b6c1
86 87 88	58	30 30a	MA	TU KU4 GUR8	a1b7
560	334	187	TC	A2	a1c6d1
86 87 88	58	30 30a	TC	TU KU4 GUR8	a1c7
583	372	214	MA MA	UZ	a2b1c5
134	79	54	NA TC MA MA	NAM	a2b1c5
141	85	60	MA	GI	a2b1c5
815	538	294	MA	KIN	a2b1c5
348	205	134	TB	IL	a2b1c5
137	81	56	MA	MUD	a2b1c5
641	399	236	MA TC	IM	a2b1c5
722	460			SU7	a2b1c5

MA = Middle Assyrian forms after ABZ and MZ₂; NA = Neo-Assyrian forms after ditto, only noted with other sigla;
SH = Cancik-Kirschbaum 1996; TC = Jakob 2009; TB = Maul 1992; TP = Weidner 1952/3

MZ₂	ABZ	AkkSyll	Sign	Name	Parameters
348	205	134	MA	IL	a2b2c3d1
503	310+311		MA	GURUN	a2b2c4
663	412	243	SH	UGU	a2b2c4
176	106	79	MA	GU2	a2b2c4
511	328	178	TC	RA	a2b2c4
182 183	113 114	86 83	MA	SU4 DAR	a2b2c4
670	418		TC	U-DAR	a2b2c4
761	487		MA	ESIR2	a2b2c4
348	205	134	TC	IL	a2b3c3
663	412	243	TC	UGU	a2b3c3
761	487			ESIR2	a2b3c3
670	418		MA	U-DAR	a2b4c2
815	538	294	MA MA TC SH	KIN	a2b4c2
511	328	178	SH	RA	a2b4c2

MA = Middle Assyrian forms after ABZ and MZ₂; NA = Neo-Assyrian forms after ditto, only noted with other sigla; SH = Cancik-Kirschbaum 1996; TC = Jakob 2009; TB = Maul 1992; TP = Weidner 1952/3

MZ₂	ABZ	AkkSyll	Sign	Name	Parameters
720 721	459 459a	267 268		DUL DU6	a2b4c2
561	335	191	SH · SH	DA	a2b4c2
740	462			KIxU HABRUD	a2b4c2
566	353	202	SH · SH TC · TC	ŠA	a2b4c2
884	555	299	NA MA	ZUM	a2b4c2
886 887 888	556 556a	300		NIN9 NIN MIM+MA	a2b4c2
464	295ee			MAŠKIM3	a2b5c1
511	328	178	SH	RA	a2b5c1
583	372	214	MA	UZ	a2b5c1
663	412	243	SH	UGU	a2b5c1
721	459a	268	MA · MA	DU6	a2b5c1
737	461	269	MA	KI	a2b5c1
259	147	109	SH	ZI2	a2b6

MA = Middle Assyrian forms after ABZ and MZ₂; NA = Neo-Assyrian forms after ditto, only noted with other sigla; SH = Cancik-Kirschbaum 1996; TC = Jakob 2009; TB = Maul 1992; TP = Weidner 1952/3

MZ$_2$	ABZ	AkkSyll	Sign	Name	Parameters
292	164	115	MA MA	SUM	a2b6
20	52		SH	ITI	a2b6
511	328	178	MA SH SH	RA	a2b6
567	354	203		ŠU+NIGIN2	a2b6
348	205	134	TC	IL	a2c5d1
583	372	214	SH TC	UZ	a2c6
561	335	191	TC	DA	a2c6
614	394			NUNUZ	a2c6
511	328	178	TC	RA	a2c6
292	164	115	SH	SUM	a2c6
566	353	202	TC	ŠA	a2c6
663	412	243	TC	UGU	a2c6
670	418		TC	U-DAR	a2c6
737	461	269	TB	KI	a2c6

MA = MIDDLE ASSYRIAN FORMS AFTER ABZ AND MZ$_2$; NA = NEO-ASSYRIAN FORMS AFTER DITTO, ONLY NOTED WITH OTHER SIGLA;
SH = CANCIK-KIRSCHBAUM 1996; TC = JAKOB 2009; TB = MAUL 1992; TP = WEIDNER 1952/3

MZ$_2$	ABZ	AkkSyll	Sign	Name	Parameters
292	164	115	MA	SUM	a2c6
815	538	294	SH	KIN	a2c6
109	63c	38		KAD3	a3b1c4
584	373	215	MA	SUD	a3b1c4
184	115	87	TC	SAG	a3b1c4
260	142a	104	SH	IA	a3b1c4
677	424	246		LIBIŠ	a3b2c3
895	554			MUNUS-LA-GAR	a3b2c3
700	443			UTU2	a3b2c3
729	454		TC	SIG5	a3b2c3
8	11	10		BUR2	a3b2c3
887	556	300	TC	NIN	a3b3c2
164	99	71	NA MA TC	ᴰ+EN	a3b3c2
8	11	10	MA	BUR2	a3b3c2
77	43	23		URU2	a3b3c2
671	419		MA	SAGŠU	a3b3c2

MA = Middle Assyrian forms after ABZ and MZ$_2$; NA = Neo-Assyrian forms after ditto, only noted with other sigla;
SH = Cancik-Kirschbaum 1996; TC = Jakob 2009; TB = Maul 1992; TP = Weidner 1952/3

MZ₂	ABZ	AkkSyll	Sign	Name	Parameters
814	537, 65+537*		(sign) (sign) MA	AD3	a3b4c1
79	44		(sign)	ASARI	a3b4c1
184	115	87	(sign) SH	SAG	a3b4c1
671	419		(sign)	SAGŠU	a3b4c1
584	373	215	(sign) MA	SUD	a3b5
812 813	537	292 293	(sign) MA	LU DIB	a3b5
248	139	102	(sign) MA	TA	a3b5
260	142a	104	(sign)	IA	a3b5
731	455	264	(sign) TC (sign) TB	U3	a3c5
729	454		(sign) TC	SIG5	a3c5
135	79a	54a	(sign)	BURU5*	a4b1c3
165	54		(sign) TC	BURU14	a4b1c3
731	455	264	(sign) SH	U3	a4b2c1d1
726	451	263	(sign)	AR	a4b2c2
590	376*	219	(sign) SH	KAR	a4b2c2
899	564	306	(sign)	EL	a4b2c2

MA = Middle Assyrian forms after ABZ and MZ₂; NA = Neo-Assyrian forms after ditto, only noted with other sigla; SH = Cancik-Kirschbaum 1996; TC = Jakob 2009; TB = Maul 1992; TP = Weidner 1952/3

MZ₂	ABZ	AkkSyll	Sign	Name	Parameters
385 386	229	143 144		NA4 DAG3	a4b2c2
491	319	170	MA	GA	a4b2c2
133	78a	53	MA	U5	a4b3c1
742	461, 280+464	269a	TC	KIMIN	a4b3c1
497	323		MA	ALAD	a4b3c1
558	346	197		GIR	a4b3c1
731	455	264	SH	U3	a4b3c1
733	456	265		HUL	a4b3c1
297	131	97	SH SH	AZ	a4b4
559	349	199	MA	BUR	a4b4
242	138	101		DUB	a4b4
434	233, 40 +230*			ŠITA2	a4b4
392	237			AMA	a4b4
745	468	272	TC	KUG	a4b4

MA = Middle Assyrian forms after ABZ and MZ₂; NA = Neo-Assyrian forms after ditto, only noted with other sigla;
SH = Cancik-Kirschbaum 1996; TC = Jakob 2009; TB = Maul 1992; TP = Weidner 1952/3

MZ₂	ABZ	AkkSyll	Sign	Name	Parameters
466	295k	154		ŠAB	a4b4
836	595	322		GIN2	a4b4
438	280+249b	151 152		DAG	a4b4
408	252			SILA4	a4b4
899	564	306		EL	a4c4
742	461, 280+464	269a		KIMIN	a4c4
590	376*	219		KAR	a4c4
385 386	229	143 144		NA4 DAG3	a4c4
111	68	41		RU	a5b1c2
381	211	138		UŠ	a5b2c1
145	87a	63a		TUR3	a5b2c1
801	528			LAGABxNIG2	a6b1c1
801	528			LAGABxNIG2	a6b2
608	390			PEŠ4	a6c2

MA = MIDDLE ASSYRIAN FORMS AFTER ABZ AND MZ₂; NA = NEO-ASSYRIAN FORMS AFTER DITTO, ONLY NOTED WITH OTHER SIGLA; SH = CANCIK-KIRSCHBAUM 1996; TC = JAKOB 2009; TB = MAUL 1992; TP = WEIDNER 1952/3

MZ₂	ABZ	AkkSyll	Sign	Name	Parameters
864 867	598d		MA	USSU	a8
336	190	128	MA	ZIG	b2c5d1
543	333	186	SH	GAR3	b2c6
176	106	79	MA	GU2	b2c6
311	171	121		UZU	b3c5
543	333	186	TC	GAR3	b3c5
336	190	128		ZIG	b4c4
543	333	186	TC	GAR3	b4c4
704	445		MA	DUGUD	b7c1
540	332	185		ZAG	b7c1
538	331c			USSU3	b8
219	125e			USSU2	b8

MA = Middle Assyrian forms after ABZ and MZ₂; NA = Neo-Assyrian forms after ditto, only noted with other sigla; SH = Cancik-Kirschbaum 1996; TC = Jakob 2009; TB = Maul 1992; TP = Weidner 1952/3

MZ$_2$	ABZ	AkkSyll	Sign	Name	Parameters
168	95	69		MUN	a1b1c6d1
564	351	200	MA NA	SIG7*	a1b1c7
514	330	180	TC	LU2	a1b1c7
252	142		SH	I+NA	a1b1c7
894	561			TUGUL	a1b1c7
168	95	69	SH	MUN	a1b2c6
168	95	69	MA	MUN	a1b3c5
252	142		SH	I+NA	a1b3c5
644	401	238	MA	HAR	a1b3c5
560	334	187	TC	A2	a1b3c5
86 87 88	58	30 30a	SH	TU KU4 GUR8	a1b3c5
352	202	133		KAŠ4	a1b3c5
313	172	122		NE	a1b4c4
296	130	96	SH	UG	a1b4c4

MA = Middle Assyrian forms after ABZ and MZ$_2$; NA = Neo-Assyrian forms after ditto, only noted with other sigla;
SH = Cancik-Kirschbaum 1996; TC = Jakob 2009; TB = Maul 1992; TP = Weidner 1952/3

MZ$_2$	ABZ	AkkSyll	Sign	Name	Parameters
560	334	187	TB TC SH	A2	a1b4c4
232	195			UNUG	a1b4c4
644	401	238	SH	HAR	a1b4c4
86 87 88	58	30 30a	MA SH	TU KU4 GUR8	a1b4c4
296	130	96	MA	UG	a1b4c4
296	130	96	MA	UG	a1b6c2
252	142		TC MA	I+NA	a1b6c2
252	142		TC	I+NA	a1b8
86 87 88	58	30 30a	MA	TU KU4 GUR8	a1b8
86 87 88	58	30 30a	TC	TU KU4 GUR8	a1c8
252	142		TC	I+NA	a1c8
134	79	54	MA	NAM	a2b1c6

MA = MIDDLE ASSYRIAN FORMS AFTER ABZ AND MZ$_2$; NA = NEO-ASSYRIAN FORMS AFTER DITTO, ONLY NOTED WITH OTHER SIGLA;
SH = CANCIK-KIRSCHBAUM 1996; TC = JAKOB 2009; TB = MAUL 1992; TP = WEIDNER 1952/3

MZ₂	ABZ	AkkSyll	Sign		Name	Parameters
670	418			MA	U-DAR	a2b2c5
85	59	31	SH	TC	LI	a2b2c5
541	331e	184	TC		SAR	a2b2c5
695	437	255	TC	TC	AMAR.UTU	a2b2c5
362	215	141	TC		ŠIM	a2b2c5
694	436	254a			LAMxKUR	a2b2c5
176	106	79	MA		GU2	a2b2c5
740	462		MA		HABRUD	a2b2c5
85	59	31	MA		LI	a2b2c5
266	151	112	TC		LUGAL	a2b3c3d1
348	205	134	TC SH		IL	a2b3c4
362	215	141		MA	ŠIM	a2b4c3
261	148	110	TC		IN	a2b4c3
886 887 888	556 556a	300	MA		NIN9 NIN NIN+MA	a2b5c2

MZ₂	ABZ	AkkSyll	Sign	Name	Parameters
815	538	294	MA MA	KIN	a2b5c2
738				KIxBAD HABRUD	a2b5c2
889	557	301		DAM	a2b5c2
554	344	195	MA	BARA2	a2b5c2
568	354b	205		KAD4	a2b5c2
29	17		MA	UŠ11	a2b5c2
91	57	29	TC	MAH	a2b5c2
884	555	299	SH	ZUM	a2b5c2
85	59	31	MA	LI	a2b5c2
29	17			UŠ11	a2b6c1
183	114	83	TP MA	DAR	a2b6c1
541	331e	184	TC	SAR	a2b6c1
275	152, 8	114	SH	BAD3	a2b6c1
21	52*			ITI2	a2b6c1
554	344	195		BARA2	a2b7

MA = MIDDLE ASSYRIAN FORMS AFTER ABZ AND MZ₂; NA = NEO-ASSYRIAN FORMS AFTER DITTO, ONLY NOTED WITH OTHER SIGLA;
SH = CANCIK-KIRSCHBAUM 1996; TC = JAKOB 2009; TB = MAUL 1992; TP = WEIDNER 1952/3

MZ$_2$	ABZ	AkkSyll	Sign	Name	Parameters
555	345	196		GUG2	a2b7
271	152	113	MA	EZEN	a2b7
541	331e	184	TC	SAR	a2b7
85	59	31	TC	LI	a2c5d2
541	331e	184	TC	SAR	a2c7
85	59	31	TC	LI	a2c7
663	412	243	TC	UGU	a2c7
292	164	115	SH	SUM	a2c7
887	556	300	TC	NIN	a2c7
611	392	225		UH2	a3b1c5
814	537, 65+537*		MA	AD3	a3b1c5
584	373	215	MA	SUD	a3b1c5
266	151	112	TC	LUGAL	a3b1c5

MA = MIDDLE ASSYRIAN FORMS AFTER ABZ AND MZ$_2$; NA = NEO-ASSYRIAN FORMS AFTER DITTO, ONLY NOTED WITH OTHER SIGLA;
SH = CANCIK-KIRSCHBAUM 1996; TC = JAKOB 2009; TB = MAUL 1992; TP = WEIDNER 1952/3

MZ₂	ABZ	AkkSyll	Sign	Name	Parameters
585	374	216		MUŠ	a3b1c5
203	122b	88a		UZ3	a3b2c2d2
261	148	110		IN	a3b2c4
418	261			ESAG2 (GA2xŠE)	a3b2c4
503	310+311			GURUN	a3b2c4
636	398	234		AH	a3b2c4
142	86	61		RI	a3b3c3
203	122b	88a		UZ3	a3b4c2
815	538	294		KIN	a3b4c2
877	550	297		HUL2	a3b4c2
61	32	19		EME	a3b5c1
30 73	17a 40			UKKIN (KAxBAR)	a3b5c1

MA = Middle Assyrian forms after ABZ and MZ₂; NA = Neo-Assyrian forms after ditto, only noted with other sigla;
SH = Cancik-Kirschbaum 1996; TC = Jakob 2009; TB = Maul 1992; TP = Weidner 1952/3

MZ$_2$	ABZ	AkkSyll	Sign	Name	Parameters
814	537, 65+537*		MA	AD3	a3b5c1
464	295f			ŠABRA	a3b5c1
247	129a	95		MUL	a3b6
467	295l			NUSKA	a3b6
61	32	19		EME	a3b6
30 73	17a			UKKIN (KAxBAR)	a3b6
584	373	215	MA	SUD	a4b1c4
514	330	180	SH	LU2	a4b1c4
150	89	66	MA	HUB	a4b1c4
707	447a			NIGIN3	a4b2c3
899	564	306	SH	EL	a4b2c3
725	450	262		PAD3	a4b2c3
731	455	264	TC	U3	a4b3c2

MA = Middle Assyrian forms after ABZ and MZ$_2$; NA = Neo-Assyrian forms after ditto, only noted with other sigla; SH = Cancik-Kirschbaum 1996; TC = Jakob 2009; TB = Maul 1992; TP = Weidner 1952/3

MZ₂	ABZ	AkkSyll	Sign	Name	Parameters
432	271			ARHUŠ	a4b3c2
899	564	306	SH	EL	a4b3c2
8	11	10	MA	BUR2	a4b3c2
898	563	305		NIG	a4b3c2
79	44		NA MA	ASARI	a4b4c1
674 675	423	245		KIR6 GIRI16	a4b4c1
297	131	97	TC	AZ	a4b4c1
731	455	264	TC MA	U3	a4b4c1
558	346	197	MA	GIR	a4b4c1
742	461, 280+ 464	269a		KIMIN	a4b4c1
468	295m	155	MA	SIPA	a4b5
297	131	97	TC	AZ	a4b5
836	595	322	MA	GIN2	a4b5
408	257		MA	SILA4	a4b5
17	8	7	MA	ŠEN	a5b1c3

MA = MIDDLE ASSYRIAN FORMS AFTER ABZ AND MZ₂; NA = NEO-ASSYRIAN FORMS AFTER DITTO, ONLY NOTED WITH OTHER SIGLA; SH = CANCIK-KIRSCHBAUM 1996; TC = JAKOB 2009; TB = MAUL 1992; TP = WEIDNER 1952/3

MZ$_2$	ABZ	AkkSyll	Sign	Name	Parameters
899	564	306	TB	EL	a5b2c2
728	449			U6	a5b3c1
17	8	7	MA	ŠEN	a5b4
899	564	306	TB	EL	a5c4
790	513			GARIM (LAGAB - x KUG)	a6b2c1
145	87a	63a		TUR3	a6b2c1
384	211b			KAŠ3	a6b2c1
489	317			UMBISAG2	a6b3
153	103	75		D+INNIN	a6b3
559	349	199	TC	BUR	a6c3
431	278			GALGA	a7b2
868	598e			ILIMMU	a9
305	166			KASKAL-BU	b1c6d2
645	402	239	MA	HUŠ	b2c6d1
696	438			SISKUR	b2c7

MA = MIDDLE ASSYRIAN FORMS AFTER ABZ AND MZ$_2$; NA = NEO-ASSYRIAN FORMS AFTER DITTO, ONLY NOTED WITH OTHER SIGLA;
SH = CANCIK-KIRSCHBAUM 1996; TC = JAKOB 2009; TB = MAUL 1992; TP = WEIDNER 1952/3

MZ$_2$	ABZ	AkkSyll	Sign	Name	Parameters
311	171	121	MA	UZU	b3c6
305	166			KASKAL-BU	b3c6
645	402	239		HUŠ	b4c5
543	333	186	MA	GAR3	b4c5
704	445			DUGUD	b8c1
539	331d			ILIMMU3	b9
220	125f			ILIMMU2	b9

MA = Middle Assyrian forms after ABZ and MZ$_2$; NA = Neo-Assyrian forms after ditto, only noted with other sigla; SH = Cancik-Kirschbaum 1996; TC = Jakob 2009; TB = Maul 1992; TP = Weidner 1952/3

MZ₂	ABZ	AkkSyll	Sign	Name	Parameters
668	416			GAKKUL	a1b1c7d1
262	149	111	MA	RAB	a1b3c6
560	334	187	MA	A2	a1b4c5
86 87 88	58	30 30a	TP	TU KU4 GUR8	a1b4c5
313	172	122	MA TC	NE	a1b4c5
232	195		MA	UNUG	a1b5c4
564	351	200	TP MA	SIG7	a1b5c4
262	149	111	MA	RAB	a1b6c3
327	184			NINDA2 - x GU4	a1b6c3
353	208		MA	ANŠE	a1b7c2
262	149	111		RAB	a1b9
134	79	54	MA TC	NAM	a2b1c7

MZ$_2$	ABZ	AkkSyll	Sign	Name	Parameters
300	168	118	MA	EDIN	a2b2c5d1
300	168	118	MA	EDIN	a2b2c6
541	331e	184	TC MA MA MA	SAR	a2b2c6
85	59	31	SH TB	LI	a2b3c5
507	326	176		GI4	a2b4c4
545	337	189	MA	MURU2	a2b5c3
670	418		MA TP	U-DAR	a2b6c2
350	206a	136		LAH4	a2b6c2
85	59	31	MA MA	LI	a2b7c1
271	152	113	SH	EZEN	a2b8
541	331e	184	MA TC	SAR	a2b8
554	344	195	MA	BARA2	a2b8
261	148	110	TC	IN	a2c7d1

MA = MIDDLE ASSYRIAN FORMS AFTER ABZ AND MZ$_2$; NA = NEO-ASSYRIAN FORMS AFTER DITTO, ONLY NOTED WITH OTHER SIGLA;
SH = CANCIK-KIRSCHBAUM 1996; TC = JAKOB 2009; TB = MAUL 1992; TP = WEIDNER 1952/3

MZ₂	ABZ	AkkSyll	Sign	Name	Parameters
541	331e	184	TB	SAR	a2c8
275	152, 8	114	TB	BAD3	a2c8
85	59	31	SH SH TC TB	LI	a2c8
585	374	216	MA	MUŠ	a3b1c6
514	330	180	TC	LU2	a3b1c6
266	151	112	SH	LUGAL	a3b1c6
636	398	234	MA	AH	a3b2c5
266	151	112	TC	LUGAL	a3b2c5
679	426			MEZE	a3b4c3
514	330	180	MA	LU2	a3b4c3
261	148	110	MA	IN	a3b4c3

MA = Middle Assyrian forms after ABZ and MZ₂; NA = Neo-Assyrian forms after ditto, only noted with other sigla;
SH = Cancik-Kirschbaum 1996; TC = Jakob 2009; TB = Maul 1992; TP = Weidner 1952/3

MZ₂	ABZ	AkkSyll	Sign	Name	Parameters
897	554, 84 + 556,8			EGI2	a3b5c2
512	329	179	MA	DUL3	a3b6c1
59				KAxIGI cf. ASARI	a3b6c1
424	265			ITIMA (GA2xMI)	a3b6c1
467	295I		MA	NUSKA	a3b7
514	330	180		LU2	a3b7
556	347	198	MA	MIR	a3b7
512	329	179		DUL3	a3b7
261	148	110	MA	IN	a3b7
127	97	70		D+AG	a3b7
261	148	110	TC	IN	a3c6d1
261	148	110	TB	IN	a3c7
585	374	216	MA	MUŠ	a4b1c5
767	491	281	SH SH	ZAR	a4b1c5

MA = Middle Assyrian forms after ABZ and MZ₂; NA = Neo-Assyrian forms after ditto, only noted with other sigla; SH = Cancik-Kirschbaum 1996; TC = Jakob 2009; TB = Maul 1992; TP = Weidner 1952/3

MZ₂	ABZ	AkkSyll	Sign	Name	Parameters
882	596+461*			PEŠ2	a4b1c5
514	330	180	TC	LU2	a4b1c5
109	63c	38	MA	KAD3	a4b1c5
816	539	295	MA MA	SIG2	a4b4c2
297	131	97	MA	AZ	a4b4c2
727	452			AGRIG	a4b5c1
731 732	455	264	NA MA SH SH	u3 LIBIR	a4b5c1
324	181			AZU	a4b5c1
297	131	97	MA	AZ	a4b6
468	295m	155		SIPA	a4b6
247	129a	95	SH	MUL	a4b6
109	63c	38	MA	KAD3	a4c5d1
731	455	264	TC	u3	a4c6
674	423	245	MA	KIR6	a5b4c1
236	200		NA MA	NINA	a5b4c1

MA = Middle Assyrian forms after ABZ and MZ₂; NA = Neo-Assyrian forms after ditto, only noted with other sigla;
SH = Cancik-Kirschbaum 1996; TC = Jakob 2009; TB = Maul 1992; TP = Weidner 1952/3

MZ₂	ABZ	AkkSyll	Sign	Name	Parameters
152	102	74		MUŠ2	a5b5
64	35	21		NAG	a5b5
731	455	264	TB	U3	a5c5
106	63d	40		KID2	a8b1c1
502	325	175		NIR	a8b2
301	169	119	MA	TAH	b2c8
643	400	237		BIR	b6c4
704	445		MA	DUGUD	b9c1

MA = MIDDLE ASSYRIAN FORMS AFTER ABZ AND MZ₂; NA = NEO-ASSYRIAN FORMS AFTER DITTO, ONLY NOTED WITH OTHER SIGLA;
SH = CANCIK-KIRSCHBAUM 1996; TC = JAKOB 2009; TB = MAUL 1992; TP = WEIDNER 1952/3

MZ$_2$	ABZ	AkkSyll	Sign	Name	Parameters
564	351	200	MA TP	SIG7	a1b1c9
905 906	567	307a	MA	SIG4 MURGU	a1b4c6
312	173	124	MA	BIL2	a1b4c6
892	569	308		SUH3	a2b2c7
85	59	31	SH	LI	a2b3c6
85	59	31	MA TB	LI	a2b4c5
545	337	189		MURU2	a2b5c4
166	100 (63*)	72	MA	DAR3	a2b5c4
509	107+327			USAN2	a2b5c4
275	152, 8	114	MA TB	BAD3	a2b7c2
275	152, 8	114		BAD3	a2b8c1
221	126f			UTTU	a2b8c1
464	295d			MAŠKIM2	a2b8c1
892	569	308	MA	SUH3	a2c8d1

MA = Middle Assyrian forms after ABZ and MZ$_2$; NA = Neo-Assyrian forms after ditto, only noted with other sigla; SH = Cancik-Kirschbaum 1996; TC = Jakob 2009; TB = Maul 1992; TP = Weidner 1952/3

MZ$_2$	ABZ	AkkSyll	Sign	Name	Parameters
85	59	31	TC	LI	a2c9
541	331e	184	TC	SAR	a2c9
261	148	110	MA SH	IN	a3b1c7
261	148	110	MA	IN	a3b2c6
178	108	80	MA	DUR	a3b4c4
84	46	23b		ŠAKIRA (URUxGU)	a3b4c4
356	209		TB	EGIR	a3b6c2
266	151	112	MA	LUGAL	a3b6c2
75	41			BANŠUR	a3b7c1
816	539	295	MA	SIG2	a3b7c1
261	148	110	MA	IN	a3b8
567	354	203		ŠU+NIGIN	a3b8
261	148	110	SH	IN	a3c7d1
535	331	182	ŠH	ŠEŠ	a4b1c6
636	398	234	SH	AH	a4b2c5

MA = MIDDLE ASSYRIAN FORMS AFTER ABZ AND MZ$_2$; NA = NEO-ASSYRIAN FORMS AFTER DITTO, ONLY NOTED WITH OTHER SIGLA; SH = CANCIK-KIRSCHBAUM 1996; TC = JAKOB 2009; TB = MAUL 1992; TP = WEIDNER 1952/3

MZ₂	ABZ	AkkSyll	Sign	Name	Parameters
131	77	51		KUN	a4b3c4
266	151	112	SH	LUGAL	a4b3c4
785	510			LAGAB-x IM	a4b3c4
129	98		MA	ME3	a4b3c4
638	398			AH-ME	a4b3c4
129 53	98 29*		MA	ME3	a4b5c2
297	131	97	TB	AZ	a4b5c2
703	421		MA	ALIM	a4b5c2
830	576			GIDIM	a4b5c2
377				BANŠUR2	a4b5c2
872	547			KUNGA	a4b6c1
767	491	281	MA	ZAR	a4b6c1
731	455	264	MA	U3	a4b6c1
468	295m	155	MA	SIPA	a4b7

MA = Middle Assyrian forms after ABZ and MZ₂; NA = Neo-Assyrian forms after ditto, only noted with other sigla;
SH = Cancik-Kirschbaum 1996; TC = Jakob 2009; TB = Maul 1992; TP = Weidner 1952/3

MZ$_2$	ABZ	AkkSyll	Sign	Name	Parameters
556	347	198		MIR	a4b7
767	491	281		ZAR	a4b7
691	434	252		TUM3	a5b4c2
858	591	318		GUG	a5b4c2
236	200		MA NA	NINA	a5b4c2
727	452		MA NA	AGRIG	a5b5c1
165	54		MA MA	BURU14	a6b3c2
65	36	21a	MA	GU7	a6b4c1
65	36	21a		GU7	a6b5
301	169	119	MA MA	TAH	b2c9
544	336	188		LIL	b3c7d1
340	192	130		GAZ	b4c7
301	169	119	MA	TAH	b5c6
689	431	250	MA	NA2	b5c6
643	400	237	MA	BIR	b6c5

MA = MIDDLE ASSYRIAN FORMS AFTER ABZ AND MZ$_2$; NA = NEO-ASSYRIAN FORMS AFTER DITTO, ONLY NOTED WITH OTHER SIGLA; SH = CANCIK-KIRSCHBAUM 1996; TC = JAKOB 2009; TB = MAUL 1992; TP = WEIDNER 1952/3

MZ$_2$	ABZ	AkkSyll	Sign	Name	Parameters
312	173	124	MA	BIL2	a1b4c7
262	149	111	MA	RAB	a1b5c6
264	150	111a		DIM3	a1b9c2
351	201	132	TB	SUHUŠ	a1b6c5
892	569	308	MA	SUH3	a2b1c9
722	460			SU7	a2b1c9
892	569	308	MA	SUH3	a2b2c8
312	173	124	TC	BIL2	a1c11
275	152, 8	114	MA	BAD3	a2b3c7
698	441a	258		DU7 DU7	a2b4c6
85	59	31	MA SH	LI	a2b4c6
464	295e			MAŠKIM	a2b5c5
507	326	176	MA	GI4	a2b5c5
545	337	189		MURU2	a2b6c4
565	352	201		DUB2	a2b8c2

MA = MIDDLE ASSYRIAN FORMS AFTER ABZ AND MZ$_2$; NA = NEO-ASSYRIAN FORMS AFTER DITTO, ONLY NOTED WITH OTHER SIGLA;
SH = CANCIK-KIRSCHBAUM 1996; TC = JAKOB 2009; TB = MAUL 1992; TP = WEIDNER 1952/3

MZ$_2$	ABZ	AkkSyll	Sign	Name	Parameters
275	152, 8	114	MA	BAD3	a2b9c1
57	31			KAxMI	a2b9c1
871	546, 6			KEŠ3	a3b3c4d2
266	151	112	SH SH	LUGAL	a3b3c6
535	331	182	MA	ŠEŠ	a3b4c5
178	108	80	MA	DUR	a3b4c5
356	209		NA MA TB	EGIR	a3b6c3
266	151	112	MA	LUGAL	a3b6c3
535	331	182		ŠEŠ	a3b7c2
816	539	295		SIG2	a3b7c2
49	26			ŠUDU3 (KAxŠU)	a3b9
266	151	112	MA	LUGAL	a3b9
261	148	110	SH	IN	a3c8d1
514	330	180	TP MA TC	LU2	a4b1c7

MA = Middle Assyrian forms after ABZ and MZ$_2$; NA = Neo-Assyrian forms after ditto, only noted with other sigla; SH = Cancik-Kirschbaum 1996; TC = Jakob 2009; TB = Maul 1992; TP = Weidner 1952/3

MZ$_2$	ABZ	AkkSyll	Sign	Name	Parameters
135	79a	54a	MA NA	BURU5	a4b1c7
261	148	110	SH	IN	a4b1c7
166	100 (63*)	72	MA	DAR3	a4b1c7
131	77	51	MA	KUN	a4b3c5
266	151	112	SH	LUGAL	a4b3c5
166	100 (63*)	72		DAR3	a4b4c4
514	330	180	MA	LU2	a4b5c3
75	41		MA	BANŠUR	a4b7c1
206	122d			SUR10	a4b7c1
556	347	198	MA	MIR	a4b8
177	107+327			USAN	a5b3c4
372	224			ŠIMxA	a5b4c3
833	577		MA	UDUG	a5b5c2
293	165	115a		NAGA	a5b7
75	41		BM 103395	BANŠUR (URU+DUB)	a5b7

MA = Middle Assyrian forms after ABZ and MZ$_2$; NA = Neo-Assyrian forms after ditto, only noted with other sigla;
SH = Cancik-Kirschbaum 1996; TC = Jakob 2009; TB = Maul 1992; TP = Weidner 1952/3

MZ$_2$	ABZ	AkkSyll	Sign	Name	Parameters
32	18*			SU6	a5b7
666	413			ŠIBIR	a6b3c3
427	270			MEN	a6b4c2
31	18			NUNDUM	a6b6
574	359			URI	a8b4
744	467	271	SH	ŠUL	a9b1c2
502	325	175	MA	NIR	a10b2
544	336	188	MA	LIL	b4c7d1

MA = MIDDLE ASSYRIAN FORMS AFTER ABZ AND MZ$_2$; NA = NEO-ASSYRIAN FORMS AFTER DITTO, ONLY NOTED WITH OTHER SIGLA;
SH = CANCIK-KIRSCHBAUM 1996; TC = JAKOB 2009; TB = MAUL 1992; TP = WEIDNER 1952/3

MZ₂	ABZ	AkkSyll	Sign	Name	Parameters
905 906	567	307a	(MA) (MA)	SIG4	a1b4c8
124	74, 238f.		(TC)	IDIGNA	a1b5c7
277	152, 4			UBARA	a2b9c2
565	352	201	(MA)	DUB2	a2b9c2
356	209		(TB)	EGIR	a3c10
806	515, 9		(MA)	NENNI	a3b2c8
646	403	240	(MA)	SUHUR	a3b4c6
816	539	295	(MA)	SIG2	a3b4c6
806	515, 9			NENNI	a3b4c6
69	34			ŠAKIRA (KAxGU)	a3b6c4
817	540			DARA4	a3b8c2
816	539	295	(MA)	SIG2	a3b9c1
330	185			NINDA2-x U2-AŠ	a3b9c1
535	331	182	(MA)	ŠEŠ	a4b1c8
266	151	112	(MA)	LUGAL	a4b3c6
569	354b	206		KAD5	a4b5c4

MA = Middle Assyrian forms after ABZ and MZ₂; NA = Neo-Assyrian forms after ditto, only noted with other sigla; SH = Cancik-Kirschbaum 1996; TC = Jakob 2009; TB = Maul 1992; TP = Weidner 1952/3

MZ₂	ABZ	AkkSyll	Sign	Name	Parameters
557	348			DUN4	a4b7c2
62	33	20		MA5; MU3 (KAxŠE3)	a4b9
556	347	198		MIR	a4b9
293	165	115a		NÁGA	a5b2c6
610	391			UD-MUNUS-HUB2	a5b2c6
373	225			ŠIMxNIG2	a6b4c3
33	19	17		PU3 (KAxKAR2)	a6b7
191	117			DILIB3	a6b7
744	467	271		ŠUL	a10b2c1
646	403	240		SUHUR	b2c10d1
646	403	240		SUHUR	b2c11
544	336	188		LIL	b2c11
97	60*			GAM3	b6c7

MA = Middle Assyrian forms after ABZ and MZ₂; NA = Neo-Assyrian forms after ditto, only noted with other sigla;
SH = Cancik-Kirschbaum 1996; TC = Jakob 2009; TB = Maul 1992; TP = Weidner 1952/3

MZ$_2$	ABZ	AkkSyll	Sign	Name	Parameters
326	183	126		AG2	a1b8c5
547	338	190		DE2	a2b5c7
278	154			EZENxGU4	a3b9c2
105	67	39	MA	GIL	a4b1c9
266	151	112	MA	LUGAL	a4b3c7
54	30	18		BUN2	a4b6c4
266	151	112	MA	LUGAL	a4b7c3
641	399	236a		IM crossed IM	a2b1c4
464	295c			RIG7	a5b6c3
293	165	115a	MA	NAGA	a6b1c7
349	205a	134a		ILxKAR2	a6b5c3
165	54		MA	BURU14	a6b6c2
284				EZENxKUG	a6b7c1
191	118		MA	DILIB3	a6b8
818	541		MA MA	EREN	a7b5c2

MA = Middle Assyrian forms after ABZ and MZ$_2$; NA = Neo-Assyrian forms after ditto, only noted with other sigla; SH = Cancik-Kirschbaum 1996; TC = Jakob 2009; TB = Maul 1992; TP = Weidner 1952/3

MZ$_2$	ABZ	AkkSyll	Sign	Name	Parameters
191	117			DILIB3	a7b7
587	375	217		TIR	a8b2c4
587	375	217		TIR	a8b6
574	359			URI	a8b6
155	103b			SED	a10b3c1

MA = Middle Assyrian forms after ABZ and MZ$_2$; NA = Neo-Assyrian forms after ditto, only noted with other sigla;
SH = Cancik-Kirschbaum 1996; TC = Jakob 2009; TB = Maul 1992; TP = Weidner 1952/3

MZ$_2$	ABZ	AkkSyll	Sign	Name	Parameters
582	371a			SIRSIR	a1b4c9d1
582	371a			SIRSIR	a1b6c8
138	82	57		SA4	a2b6c7
705	446	260		GIG	a2b6c7
676	422			LILIZ	a2b10c3
313	172, 51ff.	123		IZI-ŠUB	a4b5c6
333	187	127		ŠAM2	a4b6c5
766	494	282		U8	a4b6c5
723				LAGAR - x ŠE-SUM	a4b6c5
766	494	282		U8	a4b7c4
876	549			ŠUDUN	a5b5c3d2
876	549			ŠUDUN	a5b7c3
413	250b			GA2xSAR	a5b10
162	93			ŠINIG	a6b8c1
741 882	596			PEŠ2	a6b8c1

MA = MIDDLE ASSYRIAN FORMS AFTER ABZ AND MZ$_2$; NA = NEO-ASSYRIAN FORMS AFTER DITTO, ONLY NOTED WITH OTHER SIGLA; SH = CANCIK-KIRSCHBAUM 1996; TC = JAKOB 2009; TB = MAUL 1992; TP = WEIDNER 1952/3

MZ$_2$	ABZ	AkkSyll	Sign	Name	Parameters
179	108*	81	MA	GUN	a7b4c4
493	320	171		IL2	a7b6c2
587	375	217	MA	TIR	a8b2c5
692	434a	253		KIR7	a9b4c2
411	255	150		UR3	a11b4
646	403	240	MA MA	SUHUR	b2c13
646	403	240	MA	SUHUR	c14d1

MA = Middle Assyrian forms after ABZ and MZ$_2$; NA = Neo-Assyrian forms after ditto, only noted with other sigla; SH = Cancik-Kirschbaum 1996; TC = Jakob 2009; TB = Maul 1992; TP = Weidner 1952/3

MZ₂	ABZ	AkkSyll	Sign	Name	Parameters
326	183	126	MA	AG2	a1b8c7
264	150			DIM10 (RAB-KAM*)	a1b9c6
264	150			DIM8 (RAB-GAN)	a1b15
705	446	260		GIG	a2b7c7
903	568			LUM-ŠU2 LUM	a3b8c5
281	155			EZENxSIG7	a3b12c1
105	67	39	MA	GIL	a4b1c11
205				SUR9	a4b9c3
105	67	39	SH	GIL	a6b2c8
818	541		MA	EREN	a6b5c5
452	289			UTUL5	a6b6c4
818	541			EREN	a6b8c2
179	108*	81	MA	GUN	a7b4c5
587	375	217	MA	TIR	a10b2c4
22 23	53	26	MA	ŠUBUR ŠAH	a10b6
587	375	217	TB	TIR	a10c6

MA = Middle Assyrian forms after ABZ and MZ₂; NA = Neo-Assyrian forms after ditto, only noted with other sigla;
SH = Cancik-Kirschbaum 1996; TC = Jakob 2009; TB = Maul 1992; TP = Weidner 1952/3

MZ$_2$	ABZ	AkkSyll	Sign	Name	Parameters
124	74, 238f.			IDIGNA	a3b6c8
616	394b			LAHTAN	a3b6c8
26	16			TU6	a4b12c1
619	394c			USAN3	a5b4c8
821	544		MA	ŠEŠ2	a6b6c5
818	541		MA	EREN	a7b5c5
818	541		MA	EREN	a7b8c2
440	281a			KIŠI8	a8b6c3
449	287			UTUA	a8b6c3
22 23	53	26	MA	ŠUBUR ŠAH	a10b7
159	92a			AKKIL	a11b4c2
22 23	53	26	MA	ŠUBUR ŠAH	a12b2c3

MA = Middle Assyrian forms after ABZ and MZ$_2$; NA = Neo-Assyrian forms after ditto, only noted with other sigla;
SH = Cancik-Kirschbaum 1996; TC = Jakob 2009; TB = Maul 1992; TP = Weidner 1952/3

MZ₂	ABZ	AkkSyll	Sign	Name	Parameters
264	150			DIM11 (LUGAL-KAM*)	a3b9c6
264	150			DIM9 (LUGAL-GAN)	a3b15
821	544		MA	ŠEŠ2	a5b6c7
821	544			ŠEŠ2	a5b9c4
102	66c		MA	NUMUN2	a6b1c11
586	374, 81ff.			RI8	a6b2c10
102	66c			NUMUN2	a6b3c9
619	394c		MA NA	USAN3	a6b4c8
455	291			UBUR	a8b6c4
571	356	208		SA6	a10b6c2
587	375	217	TB	TIR	a12c6

MZ₂	ABZ	AkkSyll	Sign	Name	Parameters
124	74, 238f.		MA	IDIGNA	a3b7c10
508	326a	177		GIGI	a4b4c12
160	92b			UMBIN	a11b6c3

MA = Middle Assyrian forms after ABZ and MZ₂; NA = Neo-Assyrian forms after ditto, only noted with other sigla;
SH = Cancik-Kirschbaum 1996; TC = Jakob 2009; TB = Maul 1992; TP = Weidner 1952/3

MZ_2	ABZ	AkkSyll	Sign	Name	Parameters
573	358		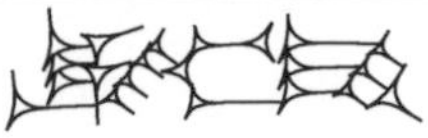	ALAM	a2b9c10

| 572 | | |  | BIŠEBA3 | a5b13c4 |
| 819 | 542 | |  | GUR7 | a7b10c7 |

907	568			SIG4 -ŠU2 SIG4	a3b8c13
460	293			AMAŠ	a9b9c6
453	290			KIŠI9	a11b10c3

| 460 | 293 | |  MA | AMAŠ | a8b9c8 |
| 460 | 293 | |  MA | AMAŠ | a8b11c6 |

| 587 | 375, 45 | | 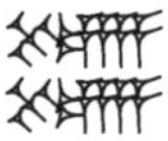 | NINI5 | a16b4c8 |

MA = MIDDLE ASSYRIAN FORMS AFTER ABZ AND MZ₂; NA = NEO-ASSYRIAN FORMS AFTER DITTO, ONLY NOTED WITH OTHER SIGLA;
SH = CANCIK-KIRSCHBAUM 1996; TC = JAKOB 2009; TB = MAUL 1992; TP = WEIDNER 1952/3

MZ$_2$	ABZ	AkkSyll	Sign	Name	Parameters
823	543			MUNŠUB2	a5b9c15d1

MZ$_2$	ABZ	AkkSyll	Sign	Name	Parameters
63				KAGUR (KAxGUR7)	a9b15c7
823	543			MUNŠUB2	a5b11c14d1

MZ$_2$	ABZ	AkkSyll	Sign	Name	Parameters
823	543			MUNŠUB2	a5b11c17

MA = Middle Assyrian forms after ABZ and MZ$_2$; NA = Neo-Assyrian forms after ditto, only noted with other sigla;
SH = Cancik-Kirschbaum 1996; TC = Jakob 2009; TB = Maul 1992; TP = Weidner 1952/3

Ebenfalls bei ISLET erschienen:

Mining the Archives. Festschrift for Christopher Walker on the Occasion of His 60th Birthday edited by Cornelia Wunsch. **Babylonische Archive** Band 1. Dresden: ISLET 2002 ISBN-10: 3980846601 (ISBN-13: 978-3-9808466-0-8) Euro 50,00

Wunsch, C.: **Urkunden zum Ehe-, Vermögens- und Erbrecht** aus verschiedenen neubabylonischen Archiven. **Babylonische Archive** Band 2. Dresden: ISLET 2003 ISBN-10: 398084661X (ISBN-13: 978-3-9808466-1-5) Euro 45,00

MacGinnis, John D.: **The Arrows of the Sun**. Armed Forces in Sippar in the First Millennium BC. with copies of the cuneiform texts by Cornelia Wunsch. **Babylonische Archive** Band 4. Dresden: ISLET 2012 ISBN 13: 978-3-9808466-5-3 Euro 40,00

Frame, G.: **The Archive of Mušēzib-Marduk**, Son of Kiribtu and Descendant of Sîn-nāṣir. A Landowner and Property Developer at Uruk in the Seventh Century B.C. **Babylonische Archive** Band 5. Dresden: ISLET 2013 ISBN 13: 978-3-9808466-7-7 Euro 40,00

Ambos, C.: **Mesopotamische Baurituale** aus dem 1. Jahrtausend v. Chr. (mit einem Beitrag von Aaron Schmitt). Dresden: ISLET 2004 ISBN-10   3980846628 (ISBN-13: 978-3-9808466-2-2) Euro 90,00

Ambos, C.: **Der König im Gefängnis** und das Neujahrsfest im Herbst. Mechanismen der Legitimation des babylonischen Herrschers im 1. Jahrtausend v. Chr. und ihre Geschichte. Dresden: ISLET 2013 ISBN 13: 978-3-9814842-9-8 Euro 60,00

Lorenz, Jürgen: **Nebukadnezar III/IV**. Die politischen Wirren nach dem Tod des Kambyses im Spiegel der Keilschrifttexte. Dresden: ISLET 2008 ISBN-10: 3980846636 (ISBN-13: 978-3-9808466-3-9) Euro 30,00

Festschrift für Gernot Wilhelm anläßlich seines 65. Geburtstages am 28. Januar 2010 herausgegeben von Jeanette C. Fincke. Dresden: ISLET 2010 ISBN-10: 3980846644 (ISBN-13: 978-3-9808-4664-6) Euro 80,00

Ancient Near Eastern Studies in Memory of Blahoslav Hruška edited by Luděk Vacín. Dresden: ISLET 2011 ISBN-10: 3980846660 (ISBN-13: 978-3-9808466-6-0) Euro 60,00